Essential Skills for a F

Book 4
Here Boy!

Step-by-step to a Stunning Recall
from your Brilliant Family Dog

Beverley Courtney

www.brilliantfamilydog.com

Books by the author

Essential Skills for a Brilliant Family Dog

Book 1 Calm Down! *Step-by-Step to a Calm, Relaxed, and Brilliant Family Dog*

Book 2 Leave It! *How to teach Amazing Impulse Control to your Brilliant Family Dog*

Book 3 Let's Go! *Enjoy Companionable Walks with your Brilliant Family Dog*

Book 4 Here Boy! *Step-by-step to a Stunning Recall from your Brilliant Family Dog*

Essential Skills for your *Growly* but Brilliant Family Dog

Book 1 Why is my Dog so Growly? *Teach your fearful, aggressive, or reactive dog confidence through understanding*

Book 2 Change for your Growly Dog! *Action steps to build confidence in your fearful, aggressive, or reactive dog*

Book 3 Calm walks with your Growly Dog *Strategies and techniques for your fearful, aggressive, or reactive dog*

www.brilliantfamilydog.com/books

Your free book is waiting for you!

Get the next piece of the puzzle

Get the second book in this series absolutely free at

www.brilliantfamilydog.com/freebook

Disclaimer

I have made every effort to make my teachings crystal clear, but we're dealing with live animals here (That's you, and your dog.) and I can't see whether you're doing it exactly right. I am unable to guarantee success, as it depends entirely on the person utilising the training programs, strategies, tools, and resources.

What I do know is that this system works!

Nothing in these books should upset or worry your dog in any way, but if your dog has a pre-existing problem of fear or aggression you should consult a force-free trainer to help. www.brilliantfamilydog.com/growly will get you started.

By the way, to simplify matters I refer to our trainee dog throughout this series as "she." "He" and "she" will both learn the exact same way. The cumbersome alternatives of "he/she" or "they" depersonalise our learner: I want her to be very real to you!

All the photos in this book are of "real" dogs – either my own, or those of students and readers (with their permission). So the reproduction quality is sometimes not the best. I have chosen the images carefully to illustrate the concepts – so we'll have to put up with some fuzziness.

Contents

Introduction

This dog is showing his owner a clean pair of heels

"Ditzy! Ditzy!! DITZY!!! C'me 'ere Ditzy. Ditzy NO!"

Ditzy didn't hear much of this. She'd heard it all before, so she carried on her merry way. "Di-i-i-itzy!"

First, she snatched a biscuit from a toddler's hand. "Ditzy come here this instant!"

Then she romped off and jumped up at an old lady who tottered backwards before being caught by a passer-by. "DITZY!"

Delight of delights - she found some fox-poo and joyfully rolled in it. "Dit-ZEE!"

Einstein said that doing the same thing over and over again and expecting different results is a sign of madness - this owner sure was mad by now!

It took several more minutes of mayhem before Ditzy had run herself out. She knew from all that shouting that her owner was cross so she slunk back slowly. She endured the lead being snapped on roughly and getting a noisy telling-off all the while.

How likely is it that Ditzy will come next time she's called?

If her owner had only realised that dogs don't come with a recall installed, that it was up to her to teach her dog to come when called, that it would be fun and only take a few minutes every day! Then the toddler would still have his biscuit, the old lady would not now be having palpitations, the owner wouldn't be in the shower trying to get the stink off her dog, and the walk would have been enjoyable instead of the embarrassing mess it became.

In other words, if she'd had this book, things would have been very different! You'll find that teaching your dog an ace, high-speed, instant, recall is not only easy, but FUN - for both of you. On top of that, you'll develop a new bond with your dog which doesn't depend on you barking orders and her (not) obeying - rather, you'll develop a companionship where both of you are reliable and consistent, and you'll enjoy your walks together.

I've been teaching force-free methods to dog-owners and puppy-owners for years, and it's a joy to watch the dog-owners change from sergeant-majors who are trying to confine and control their dog, to easy-going and relaxed - secure in the knowledge that their dog will spin on a sixpence and come barrelling back to them when they call. They and their dog have so much freedom!

So how would you like to have a bombproof recall with your dog?

If you follow the guidance in this book that's just what you'll have! This book is the fourth in a series of **Essential Skills for your Brilliant Family Dog**. It stands alone - but combined with the other three (you can find them in the Resources section) will give you a huge insight into how to get the results you want from your dog - without force, fear, or friction.

- I'll guide you through the process step-by-step

- I'll troubleshoot your training sessions so you make them as efficient as possible in the short time you have available in your busy day

- I'll show you a recall from your dog's point of view, what works, what doesn't, and why

- What progress you can expect and when

- Best of all - I'll show you how to have fun with your dog again! Isn't that why you got a dog in the first place?

If you can spend just a few minutes every day working through this program as I unfold it to you, I promise that your dog's recall will transform beyond all recognition. You'll have a dog who can come away from people, playing dogs, running children, food - even rabbits, in time!

This means you'll have a dog who enjoys far greater freedom to run and frolic.

Is this what you want for your dog? They say that the best time to plant a tree is thirty years ago, and the second-best time is today. Are you going to take the first step towards making a huge change - or carry on shouting furiously at your misbehaving dog? Are you going to get stuck into this straightforward and enjoyable program - or carry on having frustrating walks? Are you going to dazzle other dogwalkers with your dog's scintillating sharp recall - or are you going to carry on apologising to crying children and frightened old ladies, and dreading the moment when you hear screeeech-BANG as your dog races across a road?

It was having to learn the techniques to make a Brilliant Family Dog with my own busy household of multiple dogs, cats, sheep, goats, hens, and children that set me on the road to helping others do the same. I learnt early on that forcing someone to do something only resulted in grudging compliance at best; whereas getting them to participate and enjoy the process turned them into eager and fast learners. This applied equally to the dogs, the goats - and the children! The sheep and the cats not so much.

My qualifications range from the understanding of learning theory to specialist work for fearful, anxious, and growly dogs. Acquiring an anxious, growly dog of my own ensured that I learnt and understood the process of assimilating the dog into our world in a way which builds her confidence.

There are some superb teachers and advocates of force-free dog training, and you'll find those I am particularly indebted to in the Resources section at the end of this book. Some of the methods I'll be showing you are well-known in the force-free dog training community, while many have my own particular twist.

My work revolves around puppies, new rescue dogs, growly dogs - and, of course, dog owners. There are many people more gifted than I who can train animals to do astonishing things. My gift lies in being able to convey my knowledge to the dog's caregiver in a way which has them saying, "It's so obvious when you put it like that!"

Dogs are individuals and so are their owners, so sometimes creativity and imagination are needed to solve a problem. There isn't a one-size-fits-all approach to training - as you'll see when you look at the Troubleshooting sections following each lesson in the book.

And no - it's not difficult to teach. Follow the steps that I'm going to outline for you. Don't skip or jump ahead. Work on each step till it's more or less right then move on. (No need to be a perfectionist here - you don't want to get stuck.)

I suggest you read the whole book before you start so you are clear about what you need and what you are aiming for. Then re-read the lesson you're working on and go straight into your very short session. After this you can assess where you are and check the Troubleshooting for any difficulties that relate to you and your dog. Then you're ready for your next session the next day.

Straight away this book will show you just what makes a recall work and how you can get your dog onside from the start. You'll learn the force-free secrets the pro trainers use to get an instant response from their dog - without any shouting, cajoling, or mean tricks - and you'll learn the one thing that will completely change your dog's attitude to you!

Get started right now - turn your dog into a star and enjoy the process as well as the results!

Chapter 1
What you need to have and know to get success

Archi is comfy in his well-designed harness

To help you while you're working on everything you'll learn in the following chapters, I want to show you first how you can make your life a lot easier - and your dog so much more biddable. If you've read the other three books in this **Essential Skills Series** you'll know that I start each book with the tools you need for the job. Don't be tempted to skip ahead! This chapter is particularly tailored for recall work.

Treats: what and why?

Don't get hung up on the whys and wherefores of using treats in dog training. How would you feel if your boss said to you, "I know you enjoy working for me. I know you do it just to please me, so don't expect any pay this Friday!"

It's not a moral issue. It's not like giving chocolate to a child. You have to feed your dog anyway, so you may as well get some mileage out of the food. We are paying our dog for work done with good food, and - just like us - your dog will respond better to better rewards.

While I always have some dried liver or even high-quality kibble in my pocket - so that there is never a time when my dogs may not be rewarded - when I'm working with them on something new or important I bring out the heavy artillery. This means I use treats that my dog will sell her soul for, not dry kibble and pocket fluff. You can get some first-class commercial treats if you hunt very carefully, but the best treats tend to be soft, slippery, flavoursome, smelly, and home-prepared - real food in other words.

I frequently use cheese, sausage, frankfurter, pepperoni, and suchlike. You can make sardine, tuna, or liver cookies. Dehydrated meat, especially liver, is also popular, provided it's small and goes down quickly, so your dog is ready for the next reward without having to spend half an hour chewing the last one and forgetting what she earned it for.

If you're concerned about weight gain for your dog, then take out an amount equivalent to what she's earned during the day from her food bowl. If you stick to the suggestions above and give good quality food as treats you will be improving her diet too!

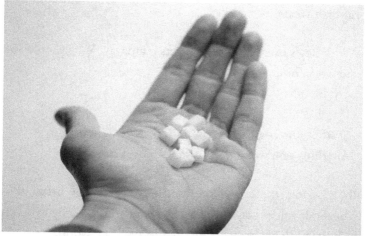

Treats need only be very small, but must be very tasty!

Good treats

- Cheese
- Sausage
- Ham
- Chicken
- Frankfurter
- Salami
- Homemade sardine, tuna, or ham cookies
- Freeze-dried 100% meat treats
- Dehydrated liver, heart, lung, etc.

…real food in other words. Ideally, they slip down quickly so your dog wants more. Cut them into small, pea-size treats.

OK treats

- High-quality grain-free commercial treats

Fairly rubbish treats

- Your dog's usual kibble - She gets it anyway. Why should she have to work for it?
- Cat biscuits
- Dog biscuits
- Stuff of unrecognisable composition sold as pet treats
- Anything you wouldn't put in your own mouth

Generally speaking, the harder the task for the dog, the better the reward needs to be. So if you're playing a training game in the kitchen you can make do with fairly ordinary treats. Out in the big bad world, with dogs and children flying around shrieking, squirrels running up trees, wind in the leaves - when you're teaching Ditzy the skills needed to come back from the child's biscuit, the old lady and the others she's previously terrorised - then you need the best stuff!

Remember this is all about choice. Your dog is choosing to do what you want instead of following her own inclination.

Control the rewards and you control the dog

Think about this: to control the rewards you have to know what your dog finds rewarding, and here I'm including not only what we can offer her but also what she finds for herself.

Here are some thoughts on what your dog may find rewarding:

- Rolling in a cowpat
- Rolling for joy
- Sniffing, tracking, air-scenting
- Running wildly
- Jumping, leaping
- Barking, singing

- Playing, tugging, tossing, catching
- Playing with other dogs - chasing, grabbing, wrestling
- Catching balls, flies, treats
- Stalking birds, dogs, toys
- Chasing balls, squirrels, dogs, rabbits, cats, scent
- Greeting dogs, people, children, family members
- Fetching the lead
- Access to the garden
- Access to the car
- Access to your bed
- Access to the sofa
- Digging, burying
- Nesting
- Toys
- Chewing

You will surely be able to add a few peculiar to your own dog! You can see from this brief list that some of these rewards will be suitable for a training session, some can be used as a big release reward, and some are not at all suitable. I think rolling in a cowpat probably comes into that category - unless your dog's due a bath anyway! And if your dog is a confirmed rabbit-killer, you wouldn't want to use the "chasing rabbits" one. Otherwise you can use all of them. Keep in mind that some of these are hardwired instinctive drives. Where possible it's good to allow your dog to practice them in a safe environment, rather than trying to squash them. Attempting to suppress these behaviours is not going to work!

Serious note: If your dog is stalking and chasing lights, reflections, torch beams, leaves, or shadows, this is an Obsessive Compulsive Disorder which will get worse - much worse, to the point where your dog may become totally disabled. You should get professional help from a qualified force-free behaviourist as soon as possible. Never use it as a reward!

Here are some examples of how you can reward your dog based on her hardwired instinctive drives:

- You may call your dog, and as she comes thundering in you turn and race away. This is a *Chase and Running Reward.*

- You may throw her toy at her as she gallops in. This is a *Jump and Catch Reward.*

- You may throw her toy behind you, race her for it then play tug with her. This is a *Chase and Tug Reward.*

- You may dance, shout, and encourage your dog to join in. This is a *Barking Reward!*

As you can see, all those rewards encourage great excitement and involvement from your dog. What better way to make a recall the most exciting thing ever?

Remember too that you need to teach your dog her recall when she's already excited, not just when she's a bit bored at home. Think about it: you're going to need her recall most when she's excited, totally distracted, and zoned in on one of her chief rewards, so that's the state of mind in which you need to practice.

You may have a session of three or four recalls in a rabbity area, then release your dog to go and hunt rabbits as a massive reward. Here's where your dog may surprise you: she may prefer to continue interacting with you and forget about the bunnies. Really!

The lesson to take away from this?

Your dog's greatest distractions are your dog's greatest rewards!

What the stylish well-behaved dog is wearing

There is not a lot of equipment you need for this, but what you do have should be of high quality and secure.

Collar

Do buy or use:

The collar should be secure though not bulky. A snap collar which is adjustable millimetre by millimetre is best - especially for fast-growing puppies - rather than a buckle collar which has fixed widths between holes. A collar is only as strong as its weakest part, so check stitching, soldering on rings, and the strength of the plastic clasp. Choose a soft-edged material that won't chafe your dog's neck. Collars should be as loose as possible while not being able to be pulled over the dog's ears - you don't want her backing out of it on a road.

Don't buy or use:

Never use anything with chains, spikes, or electronics of any kind - with the single exception of vibrating collars for deaf dogs. If you want to use any of these instruments of torture, increasingly being banned by law in many countries, you're reading the wrong book.

Harness

Do buy or use:

For attaching a long line for recalls in an area where you are worried about safety, any four-clip harness will work. The harness I personally favour is the *Wiggles Wags and Whiskers Freedom Harness*, listed in the Resources section at the end of this book along with a link to a demo video. You are not so much looking for something to prevent pulling, rather you want a harness designed to promote balance. You are looking for a harness which attaches to a double connection lead in two places - in front and on the back. You want a harness that does not impede shoulder movement, does not chafe or rub, and has the effect of balancing your dog. Look for one which has the same effect as the one shown in the video.

Don't buy or use:

Some harnesses are designed to encourage the animal to pull, like a horse in harness pulling a cart or a husky pulling a sled. They aren't unpleasant: they're just not the right tool for this job. Others are sold to prevent pulling. Sadly many of these work by hurting the dog - by cutting under the armpits or by tightening and staying tight. Not for us.

Lead

Do buy or use:

Go for a comfortable, light lead of at least 6 feet in length. It can be good quality soft webbing or pliable leather. Some people favour soft, narrow, rope leads, or plaited leather. For puppies and small dogs, you can use a puppy house line of 8 feet. You can always leave the lead attached and trailing so it's easy to catch up your dog if necessary - though not in woodland or deep cover. It may give you more confidence to let her off in the first place. If calm lead walking skills have so far eluded you and your dog, head for the third book in this series of Essential Skills, *Let's Go! Enjoy Companionable Walks with your Brilliant Family Dog.*

Don't buy or use:

Anything made with chain, spikes, thin cord, cheap leather, cheap sharp-edged webbing, anything heavy enough for a carthorse, or shorter than 6 feet.

Tag line

This is a sawn-off lead of about 8 inches in length - short enough that your dog won't trip over it. Again it's an easy way to catch her if you need to. You may well have a lead that your puppy chewed that will do nicely.

Long Line

These come in varying lengths. For ease of handling in an off-road area, 15 feet is a good length, but if you're leaving it trailing for recall purposes, 30 feet works well. Any longer and you will be doing macramé with trees, dogs, and passers-by. Connect it to the back clip on a harness, not her collar. It should be light and not absorbent - or your dog will be dragging a ton of weight after her on a rainy day!

Don't buy or use:

Extendable leads in any form. They prevent a connection between you and your dog because of the plastic handle; they are dangerous; they teach dogs to pull; and there is little control.

Now you have an understanding of rewards and how to use them, as well as what equipment you may like to use, let's get on with your training!

In this Chapter you've learnt:

- The importance of the right equipment
- How some equipment will make things worse - much worse
- Rewards are not just food - let your dog show you what she finds rewarding
- "When do I get the frankfurter?"

Chapter 2
What is a recall?

Rollo is happy to be running full speed towards me, on one call

You need to know first of all just what you expect when you call your dog.
You need to visualise the perfect recall - and that's what you'll be aiming for.

For me, the definition of a Recall is:

When I call my dog, she turns instantly and races back to me at high speed. When she arrives with me she stops and stays with me.

Picture this: your dog is mooching about in the hedgerow and you call her name.
What's the very first thing you want her to do? If you said, "come back," you're
missing a lot of subtle steps that can make or break your recall right at the start!

When I call my dog's name, I want her to turn and look at me. This may be very quickly followed by her barrelling back to me at speed, but the very first thing she did was acknowledge the call by looking at me. This is the first thing we'll be working on; getting that head-snap turn as soon as you call.

Like the sound of that? Good!

First let's have a look at some other important points.

Your brand new puppy

People often mistake their new puppy's infant clinginess for a recall. They think they don't have to train anything because their puppy already keeps close to them and comes when they call.

This will change! As your pup grows and gains confidence you will have to do battle daily with all the things she finds more exciting and stimulating than you. This will include many of the things on our list of instinctive drives, which your young dog will find irresistible. If you can start teaching the components of a mighty recall as soon as your puppy comes through the door at a few weeks old, you'll have it installed. You will be ready for when she hits adolescence around six months old and tests every boundary she sees, just like our teenagers do.

Call just once

This is one of the toughest things for owners to grasp! It works like magic once you've got it. Your dog needs to know she has but one opportunity to come and get a thumping good reward from you. The more you call, the less she will listen - just like Ditzy, whose name meant nothing to her. If you are broadcasting noise like a radio station why should she bother to come? She knows just where you are!

Calling repeatedly can also be described as nagging. Back to those teenagers again, who are expert at tuning out calls and requests - and accusing their parents of nagging them! We all know the response nagging gets in people. "Grumpy non-compliance" would sum it up. Don't do this to your dog too!

I'll show you how to get the response you want from your dog on one call. It's going to be up to you to provide the duct tape to apply to your mouth to prevent you from calling again and again.

Call Once - then Zip it!

Name versus sound

Dogs don't have a verbal language system like we do. You know how a toddler may say, "I eated it," when they're still learning the language? They've grasped the principle of the past tense but their vocabulary hasn't yet caught up.

Dogs don't have this ability to manipulate verbal language. They hear sounds, and those sounds represent things. When you say, "Sit," just as your dog is sitting, you are labelling that action as SIT. She'll recognise the sound and knows what action goes with it.

She'll also associate good or bad outcomes with that word. If every time you say, "sit," your dog gets a treat as soon as she sits, then she's going to like and respond to that word "sit." Supposing every time you say, "Sit," you abuse her and shout at her, it's not going to take long before the word "sit" has her running off to cower in a corner instead of joyfully and smartly sitting, anticipating a reward. Trainers call this a "poisoned cue". The word "sit" has come to mean very bad things for this dog.

The wrong association can happen without us realising it. You may have asked your dog to sit before an intrusive treatment - nail clipping for instance. "Sit" now means, "I'm going to do something to you that you don't like." Or, of course a rescue dog who's been mistreated in the past is going to have a lot of bad associations with a lot of common cues. You'll need to reteach her with a completely different word and only good outcomes.

So you can see from this how important it is to pair your dog's name only with good things! We all get annoyed or frustrated with others at times, whether it's our fault or theirs. If you are annoyed or frustrated with your dog, it's vital that you do not say her name! Her name is precious and should always get her heart racing and bring a smile to her mind and her face.

Here's a way to make sure she knows her name is wonderful and it's always worth responding to!

ACTION STEP Making your dog's name wonderful

1. For the next 5 days, whenever you notice your dog, say her name cheerfully - once.

2. As soon as she races to you with tail wagging - or just flickers an eyelid - reward her joyfully with a surprise - attention, fun, game, toy, or a treat.

3. Every third or fourth time she bounces to you, slip your hand softly in her collar, so she can feel the back of your hand against her neck. Don't grip hard. Then release it as you give her reward.

4. Repeat endlessly, all day long.

Speed, joy, and enthusiasm

When you call your dog, you are giving her an opportunity to race towards you and have a game. It should not signal the end of fun and freedom. When she comes back to you, she gets treats, love, fuss, and entertainment, then - more often than not - *you let her go again.*

Speed, joy, and enthusiasm - exactly what we want in a lightning-fast recall - must be built in from the start. Do whatever it takes to keep your dog lighthearted and eager to engage with you. If you need to sing and dance, then by all means do that. This will help you build a happy and enthusiastic recall - not a mopey, reluctant, slow-motion dawdle back to you.

While you don't want your dog to hit you at such speed that you are sent flying, I'd prefer that to a morose plod any day.

Follow through

When you call your dog (once!), she is going to end up at your feet. Period.

So make sure you only call her when you've got a high chance of her coming back. And if she doesn't? Don't think, "Ah well, I'll wait till she's less busy and try again." Go right up to her and call once from a yard away. She's almost certain to come then, and if not you can simply put your hand gently in her collar and call her. You're not pulling her by the collar, you are simply limiting her choices so she's more likely to choose to come to you. There's no need for crossness. She's learning.

Puppy vs. mature dog vs. new rescue dog

Your dog will respond differently according to her stage of development. I sometimes hear new puppy-owners proudly saying their dog's recall is perfect. *She's only 9 weeks old!* She's a baby - of course she wants to keep near you! Just wait till adolescence hits and your pup is adventurous and hormone-driven. You'll need a solid recall to cope with that. So use the time when your puppy responds quickly to you to build this in as a default behaviour.

I was chatting with a lady who had two dogs of about 6 and 7 years old. One of them was being particularly naughty. She said, "I can't understand why he's like this. He went to puppy classes …"

If only sending your child to kindergarten for six hours were all that was needed to educate him - it would save us a fortune in college fees!

I like Zig Ziglar's answer to this: "People often say that motivation doesn't last. Well, neither does bathing, that's why we recommend it daily."

Training your dog is an ongoing commitment which you "top up" every day.

Again like some teenagers, older dogs may have an established pattern of "selective deafness" - doing what they like when they like! Your new rescue dog will have all sorts of baggage and is unlikely to have had much friendly training. You will be building your new dog's confidence and trust at the same time as teaching her new skills. The system you are about to start on will work for these dogs just as well, but you have a bit of history to work against.

Pavlov (not the creamy meringue dessert, but the scientist)

A word about the way dogs learn:

You may have heard of Pavlov's Dogs. Pavlov was a Russian scientist who did a lot of pioneering work on the digestive system. As was common in those days, animals were used in the laboratory for testing. Pavlov used dogs. They were rigged up with a device that measured their salivation in the tests.

Pavlov noticed unexpected salivation occurring before the tests had begun. To begin with the dogs would salivate when they heard their food being prepared. Then they started salivating when the technician arrived in the building.

So Pavlov tried something new. He tried a number of sounds, including a bell. He rang the bell as the dogs were about to be fed. Sure enough - after some repetitions, they linked the sound of the bell with the anticipation of their food and pretty soon they would salivate at the sound of the bell without any food being present.

Pavlov had identified what came to be known as Classical Conditioning - the knee-jerk reaction that people have when they connect two hitherto unrelated occurrences. To us a doorbell represents a visitor and produces excitement and activity, but it's just a bell!

We can make good use of this principle to generate our astounding instant recall response! You can see now why I want you to pair your dog's name with only good things.

Dogs do what works

Dogs are simple souls. They do what works. If a certain action of theirs results in a reward - food, fun, entertainment - they'll repeat it. It's up to us to make sure that what we want them to do always results in what they perceive as a reward. It's really that simple!

It has further been proven that the predictability of that reward is key to getting consistent results. In the Marshmallow Test (detailed in the second book in this series of Essential Skills, *Leave it! How to Teach Amazing Impulse Control to your Brilliant Family Dog*) it was shown that if the tester appeared unreliable, the subjects would not comply with the testing procedure. They'd "cheat". In other words they wouldn't play ball.

If your dog finds that producing the action you want does not lead to reliable rewards, then she'll bail and not bother with this game any more. How long would you keep turning up to work on Monday morning if you only occasionally got paid on Friday? As a dog-owner, this doesn't mean your pockets have to be crammed with sausages for your dog for ever more, but it does mean that you must in some way reward your dog every single time she does what you want. We'll talk more about this later.

9 Rules for the Perfect Recall

Here's a list you can print and commit to memory for when you're out "in the field".

1. When your dog comes back to you - no matter what she's been doing or how long it took, it's the best thing she's ever done, even if you

23

need to count to 10! *The day you tell her off for returning is the day your recall will start to crumble.*

2. Always reward the recall - first-class food, toy, game, activity, enthusiasm.

3. Only call your dog when you have a 90% chance of her coming. Otherwise you are teaching her to ignore you. Close the distance and wait for the right moment.

4. Call in an exciting voice. Your voice isn't exciting? Then why should your puppy come?

5. Start indoors, then increase difficulty in small increments - different room, corridor, garden, enclosed field. Each time you move to a new area, go back to a very short distance recall.

6. When each stage is perfect, start adding distractions.

7. Nine times out of ten, call your dog, reward her - then *let her go* again.

8. When you're approaching a known run-off place, get your dog's attention beforehand. Engage her in an exciting game till you've passed the danger zone.

9. Do lots of mini-recalls in the house - whenever you notice your dog take the opportunity to reinforce her coming to you and responding to her name.

Both you and your dog should be having fun!

In this Chapter you've learnt:

- What makes dogs tick
- A little bit of science (I snuck it in there …)
- To say your dog's name only once, then zip it!
- What you may expect
- "I like this new way of thinking! I'll do anything for a sausage."

Chapter 3
Now the fun starts!

Ged the Bernese pup enjoys a game with his owner

It has to be fun. Dogs are all about fun. Make it fun and you have a willing partner. Make it "because I say so" and you will get grudging compliance, sometimes. They really aren't with us for very long - why would you want to be hard on them?

To keep up the fun, we're going to start learning our lightning-fast recall with a game. If you remember, the very first thing we're looking for is a fast head-turn.

Remember Pavlov and his Classical Conditioning from Chapter 2? He established the dogs' responses by repetition. Dogs learn by repetition and patterning just like we do. Those six puppy classes won't cut it! You interact with your dog daily - make sure your interactions are building something you want to see again and again.

As Pavlov's dogs' drooling was an unconscious response to the bell, your dog's head-turn is going to be an unconscious response to her name - a knee-jerk reaction. Just like an Olympic athlete in training, you'll be building muscle memory.

You'll be using a marker word ("Yes!") at the exact moment your dog does the thing you want her to repeat. She'll quickly learn that "Yes!" means she's done something right, earning her a reward. Then she'll start to try to get you to say, "Yes!" At that point, the training becomes totally interactive.

You can, of course, use any word you like, but "Yes!" lends itself to fast utterance. For me, it's more "Yiss!" than a sing-songy "Ye-e-e-s." If you choose "Good," you may find yourself saying "Gooo-oooo-oood!" which is way too long and has missed the moment entirely! You may use a clicker if you like - either way, the skill is in matching your sound precisely with the action you want your dog to repeat.

Learning to pay attention

Get yourself a handful of succulent and delicious treats, your dog, some good humour, three spare minutes, and a little floor space indoors. Be animated, quick, and enticing. Get your brain in gear and be absolutely ready to catch her first response! If you want your dog to focus on you, you must be able to focus on her - and focus on the outcome you're aiming for.

Lesson 1: The Focus Game

1. Stand and place a treat on the floor to the right of your foot. Your dog will eat it and possibly sniff about for more. Finding none, she'll look towards you to see if any more treats are coming.

2. Say "YES!" enthusiastically the second she turns to you and place another treat - quickly and with a flourish - to your left.

3. As your dog looks up from eating it, say "YES!" and place another treat to your right, and so on, getting into a fast rhythmic dance.

Once your dog knows the game you'll be able to throw the treat to right or left without having to bend over and place it. It's not a game of "Hunt the Treat," so be sure your dog sees where you drop it so she can grab it instantly and turn. A bowling action is better than a toss as your piece of cheese will land who knows where if you toss it.

It may take several short sessions before your dog is keen to run back and forth in front of you like a pendulum. This may take days - don't worry about a timetable. She's learning to focus on you, turning quickly to look at you after grabbing her treat. Repeat the Focus Game till it becomes totally automatic and slick for both of you - and always ends up with smiles from you and that zany expression on your dog's face.

Lesson 2: The Name Game

Now we can move forward to the Name Game. Here, we will establish that her name means a fast head-turn.

1. Start with the Focus Game, and once you have a rhythm, add your dog's name just as she's diving for the treat. She just has time to grab it and turn.

2. Say "YES!" exactly as her head turns. You are marking the muscle movement in the neck.

3. Repeat now till your dog is spinning round, ears flapping, just after you've said her name, and turning with joy and enthusiasm!

4. Stop while you're ahead! About ten treats or a minute or so is enough.

Watchpoint

Be sure you say your dog's name just as she's about to grab the treat then *follow* with "Yes!" for the head-turn, *then* toss the treat. The sequence is

> (toss treat)
> Name
> Yes!
> Treat
> Name
> Yes!
> Treat ...

Develop a rhythm and make sure these are separate events. Don't let all the steps happen at once or confusion will reign!

Troubleshooting

My dog is moving quite slowly.

Unless you have a St. Bernard or another giant breed, who naturally move their great bulk more slowly - like an ocean liner turning - then you want to aim for speed from the get-go. Be more enthusiastic! Move quickly! Inject some urgency into the game! How fast does your dog move when she sees a rabbit or squirrel to chase? That's the speed you want!

He's turning back to me, but he's staring at the food in my hands!

Good observation. This is a natural response and is quite acceptable to begin with, but you will want your dog to start looking at your face. Make sure that your hands do not move until after you've said "Yes!" If the treat is being waved about or you're holding up your hand like the Statue of Liberty, that is what your dog will focus on. Hold your hands together until after you've spoken. If your dog is still fixated on your hands, put your hands behind your back. Once they're out of sight your dog will only have your face to look at: "Yes!" Treat!

My dog's not that interested in the treats and goes sniffing for ages after she's got one.

What treats are you using? Check out the list in Chapter 1. You need treats your dog will sell her soul for. Be sure they're not crumbly as that encourages hoovering.

She's doing it, but she's not that fast.

A common mistake is to say the words at the wrong time. You only have two words to say! Be sure that you're saying your dog's name at the *exact moment she's about to grab the treat*, not after she's picked it up. Your "Yes!" is to mark the head-turn, so say it just as her head begins to turn. By the time the word is out of your mouth it'll coincide with her muscle movement. She may not be going fast because she's unsure of what she should be doing. Oh, and call her name as if she's at the end of a field. If you say it quietly because she's right next to you, she won't be learning the sound you'll use when you're out and about.

I run out of floor space when I move.

Aha! You shouldn't be moving at all. You need only stand still. It's your dog who's doing the moving!

I show her the treat each time, but she's not very fast.

Don't do that! Your treat is a reward for your dog spinning back to you, not an enticement to work. The first treat you put down is just to get her away from you. If she's already distracted you could try skipping that one and moving straight into calling her name once. You do not want to teach your dog to see the colour of your money before she'll do anything for you. Showing her the treat, waving it about in the air, putting it towards her nose, is called "Luring" and will seriously limit how far you can go with your dog. There is a huge difference between rewarding and luring. Please don't disappear down that luring rabbit hole! Keep your hands to yourself when you're playing this game. If necessary, cup your hands together until the moment you place/bowl the treat. Stand upright and just use your voice to get your result.

The treats bounce and roll under the furniture!

Glad to hear you have an enthusiastic game going! Use soft treats (see Chapter 1) and don't throw them so vigorously. You can place them either side of your feet to begin with. You only need to bowl them further away as your dog gets into a speedy rhythm.

I'm not sure she's hearing me - she's just grabbing treats.

It's essential that your dog pairs your words with her actions. This means she has to hear them, and they have to be said at the right moment. This is crucial. Project your voice a little and call her name as you would when she's 50 yards away from you in the park. That's the sound you want to associate with the head-snap! And she doesn't get a treat till you've said "Yes".

I'm getting bored.

If *you're* getting bored, what hope is there for your dog? Maybe you're going on too long. Your training sessions need only be very short - one minute to start with, three minutes at the outside - and enthralling. Five treats may be enough for some dogs. Stop while you're ahead. You want your dog's reaction at the end of a training session to be "Really? I was enjoying that!" rather than "At last. Thank goodness that's over."

She's brilliant at this game at home in the kitchen but really distracted at the park.

Too soon! Too soon to be taking the game on the road. Don't fall into the trap of testing your dog. You need to focus on teaching, not testing. Are you perhaps a male? I find that it's a boy-thing to want to test and say, "What if…" While this may make you a great and intrepid explorer, it's not what we're looking for in the nursery! Don't unravel your work before it's firmly installed! We will be building up to adding distractions, once we know this Name Game is known and loved.

All this food! I expect my dog to come because I say so.

Then you'll get a slow and intermittent recall. Everyone on the planet is concerned with *What's in it for me?* Do you go to work? Do you get a pat on the head every Friday or do you expect your employer to pay you? If he said, "I expect you to work for me because I say so," would you be back on Monday?

My dog's doing fine then gets distracted by the children or a noise outside.

Well observed. If your dog is distracted, make some attractive kissy noises to get her focus back. Don't use her name unless you can put money on her coming back to you (remember Rule 3 in the last section of Chapter 2: *Only call your dog when you have a 90% chance of her coming*). As soon as she turns and looks at you it's "Yes!" and you're back in the game. Just pick up your rhythm again from there. Having your dog focus on you when there are distractions is exactly what we're building towards.

She can do this. What next?

That's great! We will be extending this game and moving towards a real-life outdoor recall, but this is a game my own dogs love to play at any stage in their life. It's always building a firm base for your recall. So keep playing the game. We'll move in baby steps towards the perfect recall. Don't push the scaffolding away too soon!

What do I do if she wanders off?

The first thing to do is examine what *you're* doing. Try videoing with your smartphone - it may reveal you to be uninteresting and static or you may pick up the moment when your dog switches off. Is it something you said? I'd make attractive sounds - cooing or clucking, but not saying her name - to regain her focus, then tell her, "Oh dear, you missed a treat," pause for effect, then start the game again. This game is undemanding and enjoyable - don't overcomplicate it!

Taking the Name Game on the road

Once you're getting a fast and eager response indoors, you can start venturing outside with the Focus Game. You'll move on to the Name Game when you're getting the same speed, enthusiasm, and attention as you get inside.

1. Try the garden first. You need to find an area where your treats will be clearly visible. We don't want your dog to have to hunt for her rewards. Paving stones are good, or you can put down two towels or trays and buzz your treat onto them each time.

2. If your dog instantly goes mentally AWOL as soon as you go through the door, start working your way towards the open door while playing the game, until one treat is in the house and the other in the garden.

3. Remember to keep your sessions very short - two minutes max.

4. If your dog is going well and fast in the back garden, try the front of the house, perhaps your driveway or the pavement outside. Use a good length lead for this.

5. Take this gradually and always top up the enthusiasm by playing back in the house between times. Grab all those little opportunities the day presents to pick up half a dozen treats and spend them on a quick Name Game.

6. When this is all going well, you can try the park. Choose a time when it's fairly quiet, and you can find space away from everyone else to play your game. Use tree-stumps for your treats or place two towels down so she can find the rewards instantly.

Your aim is for your dog to respond automatically to her name, regardless of the distraction. Like teaching a child to swim, we only gradually move up towards the deep end of the pool as the child's confidence and ability grows. Keep to baby steps - stay in the shallow end! - but at the same time don't get bogged down and not move forward at all. The game needs to be edging forward a little all the time.

Watchpoints

If your dog has a history of running off, you may like to use a long line. To begin with you can hold the end, but as your dog becomes more invested in the game, you may let it trail on the ground. A line of 30 feet is a good length. It should be attached to the back clip of a harness rather than the collar. If you have to stamp on the line as it flies past you with a disappearing dog on the end, you don't want to put your dog in traction for a neck injury afterwards!

*   If your dog is a new rescue dog and you don't know what to expect, use the long line for safety.

*   Your dog may be fearful and tend to run away when panicked: use the long line.

When you play this game you are building in excitement and joy for your dog. There's no place for fierce name-calling, "Ah-ahs," "Nooooo," and the like. If you find yourself a bit gruff and short, then talk to your dog as if she's a toddler. Remember the Marshmallow Test - you must be consistent and reliable: she must know that responding to her name is always good.

Troubleshooting

My dog finds the grass fascinating and goes off sniffing.

Try and find a less exciting surface to play on. If your dog is sniffing before locating the treat, she may be missing your bowling action when you put the treat down. Go back to placing it with your hand and see if she gets it then. If she's taking the treat then wandering off, it may be that your treats are crumbly and encouraging her to hoover - or it may be that she finds the scents more stimulating than your game. Hmmm. Food for thought there! First, you should make your game and treats irresistible - and place them, clearly visible, on your flat surface. Second, go over and silently slip your hand in her collar, gently draw her back to where she got her treat. By now she'll be looking at you, so say, "Yes!" and bowl your next treat onto your stone or towel right next to your foot. Go back to getting the game enthusiastic indoors, then in your garden. Always aim to get a rhythm going.

In the park my dog seems very anxious about any other dogs or people. She's always been shy.

Give her some distance from the things she's worrying about. This will allow her to indulge in the game without anxiety. This game should be undiluted fun.

I've been to the park. Now what?

Go there again. Play this game daily. You want to practice some form of recall daily for ever more - even if it's only for three seconds. All my dogs get very excited when I start the Name Game with them!

In the park there are squirrels!

Squirrels are the top distraction for many dogs. Calling a dog off squirrels or rabbits takes time, but it is most certainly possible. We'll be going deeper into this in a later chapter - Chapter 5 "Taking it outside - Rabbits and other Beasts" But don't go there yet! There's so much more to learn first. For now, find a squirrel-free zone to practice. Perhaps the middle of a big field? The beach? Keep in mind that your greatest distractions will be turned to your advantage. More about that in the next Chapter!

My treats don't seem to be so attractive when we're out!

Good point: for the counter-attractions of the great outdoors you need the heavy artillery in your pocket! This leads us nicely to the next Chapter, where we'll be looking at all the things you can do to load the dice in your favour.

In this Chapter you've learnt:

- It's all games to them
- Fun is the quickest way to learn
- Dogs learn by rhythm and patterning
- "I love these bouncy games!"

Chapter 4
Four more classic recall games

Great recalls from pup and toddler!

So you and your dog are having a ball playing the games in Chapter 3: Now the Fun Starts! The games are fast, fun, and can occur at any moment in the day - not in special "training sessions." You should be getting that head snap now whenever you call your dog's name.

In this chapter, we will learn four more games designed to make the recall the high point of your dog's day. They all emphasise slightly different aspects. To start with, approach them in the order given here. in time you can mix and match. The fourth game is more challenging and will need to be taught carefully and without error, gradually increasing the level of difficulty.

First, we're going to take your head-turn further, getting a fast and furious game going! Instead of Name = Head-turn, we're now going to get Name = Head-turn and *run!*

Lesson 3: The Running Name Game

I'll explain this as simply as possible, but to help you get it going well, keep in mind your aim: Name = Head-turn and run.

1. Start your Focus Game.

2. As soon as you have a rhythm, move into your Name Game. Spend a few treats on establishing a rhythm here.

3. Now, as your dog dives for the treat and you say her name, you turn your body so you're facing away from her and run away. Keep looking over your shoulder so you can mark her head-turn with a "Yes!" as before. What's going to happen here is that as your dog turns, she'll see your backside departing - she'll run to catch up with you!

4. As she catches up, toss your treat ahead of both of you. As she dives for the treat, say her name, turn your body away from her in the other direction, watching over your shoulder so you can say, "Yes!" at the right moment. Again, throw your treat forward as she runs past you.

Get this rhythmic, fast - and fun! Play this game for a small handful of treats at least once a day, perhaps when you put the kettle on.

Troubleshooting

A snail would move faster than my dog.

You may need to run yourself to get her excited and moving. You may get away with just turning and taking a step or two away. If your dog is very small, you can run in little steps so that it looks as though you're running fast - but you're not covering much ground. This game has to be fun and enticing! Check out the quality and desirability of your treats, and when your dog last ate or rested. Be incredibly exciting for just 60 seconds! Your game should be more fun than a squirrel skittering up a tree.

She's bouncing beside me trying to snatch the treat from my hand.

Remember to keep your hands out of the way. You're not holding the treat out to her are you? *Are you?* She only gets the treat thrown as a reward for turning and racing to you. No waving the treat about to tempt her!

I'm hopeless at this - I can't dance either.

Perhaps you can use the pattern on your flooring, or the lines of the floorboards to guide you. We don't want you crashing into the wall! Line yourself up between two markers - the cupboard and the window, perhaps. You'll be turning to face the cupboard, calling your dog and turning to face the window. You need only move very little - it's the dog that's doing the running. Be enthusiastic and get her excited!

Going sideways has me tripping over.

Don't go sideways! Turn so your bum is towards your dog. The fact that you appear to be leaving will make her run faster. If you're going sideways, it's a pretty good bet you're waving your treat about at arms' length too. Turn completely away from your dog, watch over your shoulder to mark her head-turn, and keep your hands and treats to yourself.

I'm puffed out from all this running!

Make sure you're only doing a couple of steps - just enough to get your dog running - before you toss your treat and turn. Your dog should always be covering much more ground than you. Once you get a rhythm going you may just need to spin your body as if leaving to get your dog racing! *Never run ahead of your dog.*

Saying her name seems to make her slow down.

Call her name, joyfully, as you would if she were 50 yards way in a field. There's no room for a stern voice. Imagine you're calling a small child. Some people can sound a bit menacing when they say the name flatly and without enthusiasm. If you're male, you may need to go up an octave! Call excitedly! This will have her racing, tail a-wag.

Lesson 4: Puppy Pingpong

This is a great game, adored by my crew, who love to run great distances while playing it. That will come later - for now you'll be starting with - you guessed it! - a very short distance. You want your dog to have success from the start.

You need two or more people to play this game. Children love it, so you may be able to get some peace and quiet from the kids and the dog for a couple of minutes! Of course, you need to teach the children first and supervise till you know they have the game down without fighting and confusing the dog.

1. Start with two people facing each other, about four yards apart. Both people should have a handful of yummy treats.

2. Person A calls the dog *without using her name*. The reason why will become clear when you start the game. So you can call - excitedly, of course! - "Doggiedoggiedoggie!" "Here pup!" "Woo-woo-woo!" – whatever gets your dog into the game. Do *not* wave your treat about for inspection! Keep your hands to yourself. You're not luring an action: you're going to reward your dog's good choice.

3. As she runs towards Person A, he places a treat between his (own) feet. This means the dog has to run right up to the person, and not run past, run round, or - worst of all - hang about just out of arm's reach! It also means Person A won't be getting two paws amidships as the dog thunders in to him and leaps up for a reward.

4. Just as your dog is zeroing in on the treat, Person B calls her *not using her name* - "Doggiedoggiedoggie!" or whatever works for you. Now your dog has to leave someone she knows has food, to go to the person who's calling her and may not have anything. If she gets stuck staring adoringly at Person A, that person should look away, be boring, and totally ignore the dog. Person B, on the other hand, is dancing a jig and hooting happily - see why children have fun with this game? You need to play uninhibitedly! At last she'll turn and head towards Person B who will reward between his feet as before.

5. Once your dog gets the hang of this, she'll start to race between the two of you, pausing only to snatch the treat between the feet and spin back. This is excellent!

6. Now you can add her name as she's turning and running towards you. You are labelling her action of rushing towards you as "Ditzy!" - this will come to mean "run with joy and enthusiasm towards me!"

Troubleshooting

I've got a big dog. She doesn't get up much speed over four yards.

Very true: a big dog needs a larger turning circle, so as soon as you've got a rhythm going, you can take a step backwards each time your dog is heading away from you. Gradually you'll extend the distance till your dog can turn comfortably and run really fast between you - but it's important that you both start close to ensure the dog gets the game.

My puppy is small - she's getting worn out!

That sounds good! What's better than a tired and happy dog who is learning a cracking fast recall? Keep the distance between you short and the sessions equally short, just a couple of minutes. Remember to stop while she's still enthusiastic.

When I call she comes quickly, but when my husband calls she wanders slowly to him.

There can be a number of reasons for this. Women are most often the nurturers, so from the moment your puppy's eyes were open she's probably been used to females. Maybe also you are the principal carer at home, so she's not so familiar with your husband. Another thing may be that men can move more stiffly, heavily, and menacingly than women and their voices may be more suited to the boardroom or the parade ground than the nursery. Get your husband to access his inner girl and lighten up! A relaxed posture with light-hearted voice will make a big difference. He may have to make his voice higher - like when calling a small child.

When can we play this in the park?

Good question! Once you are all happy and confident in this game, and your dog is responding to her name, you can start in the park. If it's a busy day with lots of dogs and children running about, get as far as you can from the action and work the game over a very short distance. This will give your dog the best chance to succeed. If it's quiet, then you can start with a longer distance between you because there are no distractions. Always aim for success.

Where else could we play Puppy Pingpong?

If you're struggling to make time for your games - although it's only a minute or so at a time - remember a good way to play Puppy Pingpong is when one of you is slaving over a hot stove in the kitchen and the other is sitting with feet up in front of the television in the living room. (Which way round this is in your household is entirely up to you!) You'll know when to call your dog as you'll hear your partner's joyous exclamation when she arrives for her treat, so call right away. Depending on the size and layout of your house, this could be quite a long distance agility course! If there's a slippery floor where your dog needs to corner, put down a mat so that she doesn't skid and injure herself. Once you've got this working in the house, you can try with one of you in the house and the other in the garden - have fun with this!

Lesson 5: Cannonball Recall

Bella explodes forward when called

The key to a fast recall is a fast start. We've been working on that instant head-snap when your dog hears her wonderful name. So far all the games have focussed on this skill. Now, we want to go for an explosive release from whatever she's doing when you call her! If the cannonball is launched without much power, it'll dribble out of the cannon and thud to the ground. Put plenty of gunpowder behind it and it will shoot out - unstoppable - till it hits its target. When you call your dog in this game, she will burst forward with such energy that she's nearly reached you before she's started! What better - and more enjoyable - way to practice that fast recall?

Like Puppy Pingpong, you need two people for the Cannonball Recall.

1. Person A holds the dog loosely around the shoulders and chest - not by the collar or harness.

2. Person B takes a couple of steps away from the dog, maybe three or four yards at most. Turn slightly away from your dog and start to bounce excitedly to wind her up. Call out anything but her name: "Ready! Steady! Readyreadyready!"

3. Once she's looking ready to burst, Person B calls her name and starts to run away. *At the same moment* Person A, the holder, lets go of the dog.

4. She will shoot forward as though shot from a cannon. Person B is by now racing away with dog in hot pursuit.

5. When your dog catches up, reward her with a treat, a game with a toy, or even rolling on the ground with her!

This game always results in laughter and joy all round!

Two brothers play the Cannonball Recall with their puppy Cai

Troubleshooting

My dog backs out of the holder's embrace and bursts forward before I'm ready to call her.

That sounds like a good problem to have! Either the dog is not happy with the person who's holding her or she's desperate to get to you. Try and get your name call to coincide with her moment of escape - then run.

If I call and the holder doesn't let go, she won't come at all.

It's the caller (Person B) who decides when the dog is ready to explode forward. The holder only has to let go as soon as he hears the dog's name. Try not to miss the moment or your dog will get confused. You will actually be teaching her *not* to come when she's called. Oops.

I really can't run very well and definitely not fast.

That's ok. Once you've got the game going and understood, you can start a bit further out from your dog so you're getting a head start. When she starts towards you, turn and run on the spot pumping your elbows, in slow motion if necessary, so that it looks as though you're getting away. This game is a "Chase and Running Reward" game (see Chapter 1 on instinctive drives: *"Control the rewards and you control the dog"*). It adds urgency to your dog's response. You want the sound of your dog's name to elicit a head-snap turn, followed by an explosive bound and then a race to catch you up. If you can establish this, you'll find that when you call, your dog is halfway back to you without realising what's happening!

My dog is too excited to take the treat!

It sounds as if you're playing the game with huge enthusiasm, and his reward is chasing, catching, or overtaking you. This is brilliant, but you do need your dog to stop when he joins you. Maybe a favourite toy for him to latch on to?

I have to waggle the toy or treat around in my hand to get her to focus on me before I call her.

Don't let your dog decide whether or not she's going to come to you! If you show her the reward first, you give her the option of saying, "Nah, don't think I'll bother." Start much closer, sound much more exciting, and look much more active. Do very short, very quick Cannonball Recalls - perhaps as close as two yards - till she's got the idea.

My dog comes alright, but it's not what you'd call fast.

If your dog is a large and heavy breed, old, infirm, or overweight, you can't expect huge speed. What speed does he take off at when he sees a squirrel? A cat? Hears his dinner bowl clattering? That's the speed you want for your recall - always. You need to inject excitement into this chase game! Bounce on the spot and try calling as if the house is on fire - "ROVER!!!!!!!!!" This is no time for a subdued genteel voice.

Lesson 6: Torpedo Recall

Foodie-dog Lacy races towards me, flying by her bowl of food

Now you've got your dog spinning round when she hears her name. She's bursting to get to you, and she flies as fast as she can to catch up with you. We're going to add a bit of real life to the mix in the form of distraction. While the Cannonball Recall focusses on an explosive response, the Torpedo Recall is about your dog taking a straight line to you, without deviation!

To play the Torpedo Recall game, you need to know exactly how attractive various distractions are to your dog. You can list them and number them so that your dog's top distraction is something you'll gradually work up to.

For one of my dogs - Coco - any person or child within sight is a big distraction. If a person is walking towards us saying, "Hello," and gesturing excitedly, we are at Number One on Coco's personal distraction list: he's desperate to meet them and wiggle about at their feet.

For another of my dogs - Lacylu - food is a major distraction.

For Rollo the Border Collie it's seeing anything move: a broom sweeping, flies buzzing, a ball being thrown, and people running.

For Cricket the Whippet it's the tiniest movement in the undergrowth which suggests - bunnies!

You can see there's quite a list of major distractions in my household! Hence my head tends to spin on dog walks like a radar scanner checking out the distractions before they cause a problem. Make your own individual list, and we'll gradually inoculate your dog against the things that currently completely derail her brain.

Just a note: If your dog will stay where you put her for a moment you can play this game solo. Otherwise you'll need a helper to gently hold her till you're ready.

1. Practice a couple of straightforward, joyous, recalls as a warm-up.

2. Now take a very watered-down version of your dog's distraction, perhaps Number Ten on your list. For Coco this could be a person standing still, facing away, at a distance. For Lacylu, it's an empty food packet or bowl. Rollo's sheepdog eye will be caught by anything that may move fast, so just a ball lying on the ground would be enough of a challenge for him. Cricket the bunny-hunter could be 100 yards from the nearest hedge or tree.

3. Make a triangular pattern with your dog on one corner, you on another corner, and the distraction at the third point. *This is not an equilateral triangle!* You could be 5 yards from your dog, and the distraction could be 50 yards away.

4. Call your dog to you and reward with enthusiasm with a treat or game, *then race together* to the distraction which she ignored, letting her interact with it: let social butterfly greet the person; give foodie dog another treat as if from the packet on the ground; throw the ball; allow rabbity dog a moment of snuffling in the undergrowth.

5. Repeat, with the distraction a little nearer.

6. Repeat, with it even closer.

7. Keep going till your dog has to swerve round the distraction to reach you. This may take you a month of practice! Don't make it too hard too soon!

Troubleshooting

I park my dog with a "holder" and walk away, but she only has eyes for the food bowl miles away.

You've clearly chosen the right distraction! She needs to be focussed at least partially on you before you call. Engage your dog before you leave her - dance about, move only a couple of yards away, then - while she's still looking at you - call excitedly, turn, and run. Your triangle may become a very weird shape, with you calling her and running in the opposite direction from the distraction. You can leave the food bowl empty, then fling a treat in as you both get there after your recall. That way, if she should make a mistake, she'll find a disappointingly empty bowl. The only way the bowl will "pay" is by getting there via you.

As soon as I call her, and my friend lets go, my dog races straight to the distraction.

The distraction is too close, and you're not getting your pup's attention before you call. You can put the distraction further away - or position it behind your friend who's holding the dog - and you stay very close to call her to you. When she's reached you and claimed her reward, you can then shoot off with her to the distraction. You don't want your dog claiming the prize without permission. So if it's a food bowl distraction, the bowl is empty till you get there with the food; if it's a toy distraction, try hanging it over a high branch so she can't get it till you're there; if it's a person distraction, the person can refuse to interact with the dog unless you arrive with her.

My dog's bonkers. She can't sit still for me to call her.

Try with a friend holding her, like for the Cannonball Recall. Be as quick as you can setting her up, leaving, then calling. You can stretch out the time between leaving her and calling her once she's got the idea. Don't forget to race with enthusiasm to the distraction once she's arrived with you.

My dog doesn't pay attention till I've called her several times.

Remember "Call just once" from Chapter 2? Each time you repeat the call you are hammering another nail into the coffin of your recall. You are teaching your dog to ignore you until you stop. Call just once - excitedly. If she doesn't respond you can go back to her and re-set her. Keep her focus from the moment the game begins, and always move fast!

My dog comes straight to me brilliantly, but then she beats me to the distraction.

This is excellent enthusiasm and you've clearly chosen a great reward for her. Catch her collar when she arrives with you or leave a lead trailing from her collar for you to catch up. Now you can run *together* to her reward.

My dog doesn't even notice the distraction.

Either your distraction isn't hitting the spot or it's too far away. You can approach the bowl/toy/person yourself before you call her, to draw her attention to it. Then run back to her, step away a couple of yards and call.

My dog started out well, but after a while she gets bored.

Boredom is the antithesis of fun training! As soon as she's played the game well a couple of times, move on to something else. Also, be sure that the distraction really is her favourite thing on earth. If she's a foodie dog and she gets a tasty morsel thrown in the bowl when you both race towards it, why would she be bored?

I'm not getting enthusiasm.

Then I think your dog may be a little confused. You haven't been telling her off, have you? This may have the effect of rooting her to the spot, unsure of what she's meant to do. Make it crystal clear, aim for success - even if your distraction has to be almost in the next parish to begin with - and only gradually make it harder. You would do well to go back to the Running Name Game to rebuild her confidence that she can do it right.

Distractions and Distance

Not a game, but two very important Ds to incorporate into your training as you go. The key is to only ever add one at a time. So if you're in the park and it's nice and quiet, try calling your dog from a good distance, then from a shorter distance, then perhaps from a greater distance. If the park is busy and full of activity, then it's a time for very short recalls.

Don't ask too much at once! Remember you're always aiming for success - you're teaching, not testing.

In this chapter we've learnt:

- Making everything a game is the quickest way for your dog to learn
- Four great recall games
- "Pavlov is on your shoulder" - get a knee-jerk reaction to your call
- "When I'm called I get the opportunity to run as fast as I can!"

Chapter 5
Taking it outside - rabbits and other beasts

What's caught Saxon's eye?

As detailed in Chapter 1 *"Control the rewards and you control the dog"*, you need to work against your dog's biggest distractions, and where possible, make them a reward. Some distractions, clearly, cannot be offered as a reward!

When I'm in a safe place - where I'm familiar with the terrain and the boundaries, and we're far from roads - and I have called Cricket the Whippet back from a rabbit hunt successfully a number of times, I'll tell her, "Off you go!" and release her as a reward. If she chooses to go and hunt rabbits that's fine, but most often she will start out, then decide that she'd rather stay with us. (She never actually catches one, you understand - it's just the fun of the hunt. I wouldn't use this as a reward if I had a chasing-killing dog.) You can adopt the same strategy with quite a few other rewards too.

- The children are playing ball in the garden, and your dog is desperate to join them. Call her to you, tell her how good she is - then let her out to join them.

- There are friendly dogs playing at the park while you're on a walk, and your dog hauls you along on the lead, trying to get to them. Call her once and make a huge fuss of her when she focusses on you. Then tell her "Go play!" and release her to play.

- Your dog is merrily digging a crater in your flowerbed. Call her, reward her warmly for coming to you, then run to the spot you have chosen for her to dig in - you can partially bury some plastic bottles and the like there, and encourage her to dig. This is a perfect reward for a digger.

As you can see, Impulse Control is a major factor in all these situations. You can learn all about impulse control in the second book in this series of Essential Skills,

Leave it! How to teach Amazing Impulse Control to your Brilliant Family Dog.

What you're doing in these games is giving the dog a choice. The right choice will earn her what she's telling you she wants - plus a treat or two and your pleasure. Choice is as important in a head-snapping recall as it is in the rest of your dog's life. What we're teaching here is for her always to make the right choice - and that is to come when called!

Those squirrels!

Remember if you don't want your dog to develop a habit, you mustn't let her practice doing it!

Practice makes perfect - whether it's something you want or something you don't want.

If every time you get to the park, your dog bolts to the trees to look for squirrels, don't watch her and complain she's at it again. This is reminiscent of Ditzy's owner, expecting - miraculously - a different outcome. Fetch her, take her gently away from the squirrelly area, and engage her with a thrilling game of speed with you. You're not speedy? That's ok - just learn how to throw a frisbee and teach her how to catch!

Working your recall to the level that allows you to call your dog away from her greatest fixation will take time. This is why you want to start simply and work up. And it's why you want to get your games "classically conditioned" - an automatic response. Just like Pavlov's dogs licking their lips in anticipation of food when the bell was rung, your dog's name should have the same visceral effect. When I called people-crazy Coco the other day, in full flight towards a walker, his reaction was dramatic. It was as if the power drained out of his legs for a moment, as he stopped suddenly, turned, and whizzed back to me at high speed. He didn't have to think about this - it just happened. He's probably still wondering how!

Perhaps your dog is mad for squirrels? Try a squirrel-free area for your walks - perhaps the beach or the middle of a field? - and have her on a lead or long line attached to her harness when you have to be in Squirrelville. You'll be able to practise your recalls in the squirrel-free zone, and gradually you will be able to call her back on your walks through the forests too.

Don't expect too much too soon, Softly, softly, catchee monkey. This is a gradual process of repeatedly getting it right. With practice and consistency it will become automatic. If it all goes wrong, don't throw your hands in the air and give up! You just need to go back a step or two and reinforce what you've already taught, showing your dog that you expect the same response in any situation.

Recall training - like all dog training, really - goes on for the whole of the dog's life. You don't go to those six puppy classes and stop training! The intensive training will ease off, but refresher courses are always good. Spontaneous daily training, interspersed with your normal life, should become automatic. At what age do you stop helping and advising your children to make the best of their life? 6? 19? 32? Never? So it is with our dogs. We want them to have the best, most enjoyable, and freest life possible. We never stop interacting with them. We never stop teaching them.

In this Chapter you've learnt:

- The magic of the right and well-timed reward
- Knowing what your dog thinks is a reward
- Using a distraction as a reward
- "I'm glad I can still dig when I want to."

Conclusion
The end of this road - but the beginning of your journey

If you've been working along as you read this book, you'll already have noticed a huge improvement in your dog's recall! Congratulations! Now you see how well it works, you just have to keep it going - regularly.

You are now able to look forward to walks without stress and without the danger of your dog landing in all kinds of trouble. You are no longer shouting, getting cross, and asking yourself, "Whose idea was it to get a dog?" Even Ditzy and her owner will be able to go for a nice, pleasurable walk once they've worked through this book!

You'll be building gradually, keeping in mind that you're going through a complete re-training phase with older puppies and dogs - and rescue dogs who have entered your life with history. If you're lucky enough to be starting this with your brand-new puppy you'll never have to re-train! You'll have it right from the start.

So while this is going to be the new habit, give your dog time to remember each time what she's meant to do. Keep those rewards flowing freely whenever she does something you like!

Recalls and related things

You may think that to get a sparkling recall, every time, you need to practice millions of recalls out in the big wild world. You're partly right.

You do need to practice lots of recalls when your dog is in an excited state. It's no use having a perfect recall when there's absolutely nothing else for your dog to do! As you've seen, the foundations need to be laid in a distraction-free area - such as your home first - and gradually introduced to the wild. As you learn together, there are other experiences which may at first appear unrelated, but those experiences are actually a great help in the formation of your brilliant, fast, recall.

Reading the four books in this series of Essential Skills for a Brilliant Family Dog - and following the guidance *and* doing the work! - will give you everything you need for *your* Brilliant Family Dog! Once you have these four key pieces in place everything else will follow naturally. You will have built such value for what you do and what you want that your dog will happily learn, all her life. Once you have studied your dog and you know what is rewarding to her, you have the key to her heart.

Book 1. Calm Down! Step-by-Step to a Calm, Relaxed, and Brilliant Family Dog

Take a look at the first book in this series, *Calm Down! Step-by-Step to a Calm, Relaxed, and Brilliant Family Dog.* There you'll discover how to teach your dog to settle on a mat in a relaxed state - an off-switch for your dog! You'll also find out how to teach your dog when she may come off her mat, so she doesn't just wander off when she feels like it.

A mat is amazingly useful for your recall! You'll be able to park your dog without a helper to hold her - then walk or run away and call her from ever-increasing distances. Now you have a whole new dimension to enhance your recall work.

Remember to keep your dog's focus when you leave her parked for a recall. If she's looking everywhere but at you - then that's probably where she'll head when she's released! So be sure she remembers where she should be focussed while you depart.

And be sure to keep your different exercises "clean." If you take the mat outside and get poor matwork - not the sparkling attention and accuracy you've trained indoors - then stop mixing it up with anything else and go back to basics to re-establish the foundation skills. If you mix a poorly-executed game with a good one, you're more likely to spoil the good game than improve the poor one! It's all about the dog's attitude. If it's sloppy in one, then she'll think it's ok to be sloppy in the other.

It's ok! You'll get there, but observe what's happening on the way and never be afraid to go "backwards" in order to accelerate forwards.

Book 2. Leave it! How to teach Amazing Impulse Control to your Brilliant Family Dog

Here's another huge helper - and, of course, not just for recalls. Let this permeate all of your daily life with your dog, so she learns to think before she acts; she learns that all her actions have a consequence - some better than others; and she learns that she can earn greater freedom by exerting self-control. With proper impulse control, she won't have to be put away when you're eating or when visitors come, for instance, or kept on the lead all the time.

You'll be glad to know that there is a whole book devoted to this amazing and essential skill: *Leave it! How to teach Amazing Impulse Control to your Brilliant Family Dog.* In this book you'll learn how to amaze your friends with your dog's brilliant decisions. Just recently, Kelly told me proudly how she had taken her 15-week-old puppy Lottie to a pub lunch. Her family could not believe that Lottie was so well behaved! Lottie stayed on her mat the entire time, continually making good choices. She did not jump up, whine, nag, pester, steal food or any of the other things people might expect from such a young puppy.

Once your dog learns that it's all about choice - the choice she makes - you're halfway to training anything you want!

Book 3. Let's Go! Enjoy Companionable Walks with your Brilliant Family Dog

Why is walking nicely on the lead essential for your recall? It develops a mutual trust and tolerance between you and your dog which will spill over into all your life together. Reading *Let's Go! Enjoy Companionable Walks with your Brilliant Family Dog* will also teach you a whole lot about how force-free pro trainers use the lead to interact with their dog - and it's not by pulling or jerking it!

As with all these books, there are - sometimes surprising - parallels with working with your family and your colleagues. Learning Theory is not confined to quadrupeds, sea creatures, and birds - we humans are animals too, and we respond in exactly the same way!

It's a combination of the Recall games I've shown you here, and the Impulse Control you can learn from *Leave it! How to teach Amazing Impulse Control to your Brilliant Family Dog,* that allow me to call my Whippet, Cricket, off rabbits!

Whippets are the sprinters of the dog world - weight for weight, they are faster than both a racehorse and a greyhound, covering 200 yards in 12 seconds. That's a staggering 16 yards per second - 40 miles per hour. They are also bred specifically to catch hares and rabbits. You can see that if your recall is wobbly, then your Whippet could be under a car hundreds of yards away before you've got her name out of your mouth.

Appreciation

I want to offer thanks to all those who have helped me get where I am with my dogs:

- First of all, my own long-suffering dogs! They have taught me so much when I've taken the time to listen.

- My students, who have shown me how they learn best, enabling me to give them what they need to know in a way that works for them.

- Some legendary teachers, principal amongst them: Sue Ailsby, Leslie McDevitt, Grisha Stewart, Susan Garrett. I wholeheartedly recommend them. They are trailblazers.

Resources

If you've enjoyed learning this key skill and you want to find the other three parts of the puzzle, go to www.brilliantfamilydog.com/books and pick up your next book!

Calm Down! *Step-by-Step to a Calm, Relaxed, and Brilliant Family Dog - Book 1*

Leave It! *How to teach Amazing Impulse Control to your Brilliant Family Dog - Book 2*

Let's Go! *Enjoy Companionable Walks with your Brilliant Family Dog - Book 3*

These cover the four skills you need to turn your wild puppy into your Brilliant Family Dog.

For a limited time, you can get the complete second book in this series absolutely free! Go to www.brilliantfamilydog.com/freebook and you will be reading it in just a few minutes.

And if you've got any specific queries, you can email me direct at beverley@brilliantfamilydog.com This will come straight to my personal inbox and I'll answer you - usually within 48 hours. Try me!

Meanwhile, for more free training, go to www.brilliantfamilydog.com and get a series of instructional emails on common day-to-day problems, like jumping up, chewing, barking, and so on.

I am really enjoying your tips which you are sending me. *Maggie and Dottie*

Many thanks for all your tips. They have really helped with my Jack Russell x Chihuahua puppy. *Melanie and Lola*

I read your regular emails with interest having attended your puppy training sessions with our Shih Tzu Molly - she is a wonderful well-adapted dog who benefitted a lot (as did we!) from your training. *Una and Molly*

I am very much enjoying and appreciating your emails. *Alex and her spaniel*

Thank you for your recent emails and keeping us updated, and for sharing your easy to follow tips, helping us to help Smidge become our Brilliant Family Dog! *Janet and Smidge*

Works consulted for Chapter 2

http://www.nobelprize.org/nobel_prizes/medicine/laureates/1904/pavlov-bio.html accessed 2015

http://psychology.about.com/od/classicalconditioning/a/pavlovs-dogs.htm accessed 2015

Mischel, W., et al. (1989). *Delay of gratification in children.* Science, 24 4 (4907), 933–938

https://www.apa.org/helpcenter/willpower-gratification.pdf accessed 2015

Casey, B. J., et al. (2011). *Behavioral and neural correlates of delay of gratification 40 years later.* Proceedings of the National Academy of Sciences, 10 8 (36), 14998–15003

Harness

www.goodfordogs.co.uk/products for UK and Europe (see video)

I supply these harnesses to the British Isles and Europe. If you get one through me I will benefit financially - but it won't cost you any more. Watch the video. If you can find another harness that has the same effect, go for it!

http://2houndswholesale.com/Where-to-Buy.html for the rest of the world

Your free book is waiting for you!

Get the next piece of the puzzle

Get the second book in this series absolutely free at

www.brilliantfamilydog.com/freebook

About the author

I've been training dogs for many years. First for competitive dog sports and over time to be stellar family pets. For most of my life, I've lived with up to four dogs, so I'm well used to getting a multi-dog household to run smoothly. It soon became clear that a force-free approach was by far the most successful, effective, and rewarding for me and the dogs. I've done the necessary studying for my various qualifications - for rehab of anxious and fearful "aggressive" dogs, early puppy development, and learning theory and its practical applications. I am continually studying and learning this endlessly amazing subject!

There are some superb teachers and advocates of force-free dog training, and you'll find those I am particularly indebted to in the Resources Section. Some of the methods I show you are well-known in the force-free dog training community, while many have my own particular twist.

A lot of my learning has come through the Puppy Classes, Puppy Walks, and Starter Classes I teach. These dog-owners are not looking for competition-standard training; they just want a Brilliant Family Dog they can take anywhere. Working with real dogs and their real owners keeps me humble - and resourceful! It's no good being brilliant at training dogs if you can't convey this enthusiasm and knowledge to the person the dog has to live with. So I'm grateful for everything my students have taught me about how they learn best.

Beverley Courtney BA(Hons) CBATI CAP2 MAPDT(UK) PPG